To Michael and Lily, and all the other children
around the world with whom I have had fun
playing games —O. D.

To Jessica, with love —S. W.

Henry Holt and Company, LLC
Publishers since 1866
115 West 18th Street
New York, New York 10011
Henry Holt is a registered trademark of Henry Holt and Company, LLC

Text copyright © 2000 by Opal Dunn
Illustrations copyright © 2000 by Susan Winter
Music arranged by Margaret Lion
All rights reserved.
First published in the United States in 2000 by Henry Holt and Company, LLC.
Published in Canada by Fitzhenry & Whiteside Ltd., 195 Allstate Parkway, Markham, Ontario L3R 4T8.

Originally published in 2000 in the United Kingdom by Frances Lincoln Limited under the title *Acker Backa BOO!*

Library of Congress Cataloging-in-Publication Data
Dunn, Opal.
Acka backa boo!: playground games from around the world / Opal Dunn;
illustrated by Susan Winter.
p.   cm.
Includes Index.
1. Games. 2. Playgrounds. I. Winter, Susan, ill. II. Title.
GV1201.D85 2000 796—dc21 99-58509

ISBN 0-8050-6424-9

First American Edition—2000

Printed in Hong Kong

1 3 5 7 9 10 8 6 4 2

Acka Backa BOO!

Playground Games from Around the World

Opal Dunn

Illustrated by Susan Winter

Henry Holt and Company • New York

Contents

Dear Parents, Teachers, and Caregivers,

Can you remember the excitement and fun you had playing games when you were young? Children love games and they will happily play a game again and again, without getting bored. Within the confines of a game, they feel secure since they know what to expect.

Games, like stories, are powerful teaching experiences. The games in *Acka Backa BOO!* are accompanied by simple rhymes, which help develop children's understanding of language and its sounds. This in turn speeds up the process of learning to read; beginning readers soon discover they can read rhymes they know well. Although this is "memory reading," it is an important step toward becoming a fluent reader, as it helps to motivate the child and build self-confidence.

Games provide many informal opportunities to teach values and attitudes. Through them you can convey concepts such as fair play, being a good loser, having courage and self-control, and sharing with and thinking of others. Games involve decision-making as well as physical and emotional participation. As they play, children learn by doing, and at the same time they learn how to learn.

Children learn by imitating and copying, so your example in playing with them provides an important role model. Young children want to please their parents and the adults they love, and it is through seeking your positive reactions that they find out about right and wrong and what is expected of them.

My selection of games is global, because I think it is important for children to grow up knowing that they can feel the same emotions as children in other countries and societies, and can even use some of the same language. Games can provide a link in global understanding on which adults can build, and I hope that this book will start you off!

Have fun!

Opal Dunn

Introduction

Every game in this book has a simple rhyme or song to accompany it. Instructions for adults on how to play are also included and most games are illustrated.

Many traditional games are global. They have traveled across continents and been adapted along the way, so often their origin is unclear. The countries in which these games are played have been listed. They may be played in other countries too and some of them may already be familiar to you.

Easy-Peasy Games

We selected these games to help preschool-age children learn about games and how to play them. Children have to discover that games are different from free play. It takes time to understand a game, so as you play together, keep explaining the goal and the rules. At first children might find it hard to accept that rules cannot be changed and they may try to negotiate. Learning about winners and losers can sometimes be a little painful to begin with, so make sure that, next time they play, you give them a chance to win. Once children have grasped how to play and their concentration has developed, try to extend games they already know or introduce a new Easy-Peasy game.

You're It! Games

The goal of these games is to find one person to have a turn, be a catcher, or just be the winner. The games provide an excellent way to make a fair decision that avoids discussion. Counting corresponds to the beats in the rhyme and is confirmed by a tap or the pointing of a finger.

Hands and Feet Games

These games give children an opportunity to compete with themselves and each other, and to monitor their own improvement. Through games, children learn how to be honest with themselves and how to identify their weak points as well as their strengths. They find out that by sticking with something, they can improve a skill. In this way they learn to accept a challenge and face it with confidence.

Catching Games

Children find these games fun and exciting, as they know that the fantasy, danger, and stress are confined. Through the games, they learn survival techniques, how to act heroically, and how to manage themselves in order to escape or, if they want, be caught. For many children these games are important because they provide a respite from the stresses and worries of their everyday lives.

Ball Games

These games involve the physical skill of handling a ball. Teach the child how to use the ball first and then introduce the game. Start with a large ball and reduce the size as the child's skill increases. If you are worried about balls, use beanbags instead. In the early years, girls often have better ball skills than boys; they also tend to practice more by themselves.

Hide-and-Seek Games

Most of these games are played in the same way with a hider, a seeker, and a safe home base. Children love these games and are ready to play from quite an early age, if the surroundings are familiar. Young children have to learn where and how to hide effectively and often need your advice.

Clap, Skip, and Jump Games

All of these games have very strong beats, which regulate the rhythm and help children keep time. When playing the skipping games, turn the rope yourself at first, as children may find this difficult. Young children find it easier to learn the actions first, then the rhyme.

Singing Games

These games can be played with children of all ages, or with the whole family on special occasions. When you introduce a game, it may be easier to begin by humming the tune and clapping to the rhythm. Once the children are confident, add the words and actions of the song. Music can be found on pages 42–43.

Easy-Peasy Games

Wolf, Wolf, where are you?

One child is the Wolf. The other children run up to him saying the first two lines of the rhyme. The Wolf replies with the next three lines, while pretending to put on his clothes. Then he shouts, "I'm COMING!" and chases the children. The first one caught becomes the Wolf next time.

France, Switzerland

Andar, Bahar

The children stand inside a circle of chalk or twigs. The leader shouts, "*Andar* (inside)," and the children jump inside the circle, or "*Bahar* (outside)," and they jump outside. The leader continues, getting faster and faster. If she shouts "*Andar*" when the children are already inside the circle, or "*Bahar*" when they are already outside, they must freeze. Children who do not follow the commands correctly are out.

India (Hindi)

Wolf, Wolf, where are you?
Can you hear me?

I'm putting on my sweater,
I'm putting on my trousers,
I'm putting on my socks,
I'm COMING!

Andar (inside),
Bahar (outside),
Andar, Bahar,
Andar, Bahar,
BAHAR.

Stroke the baby,
Stroke the baby.
Guess who did it!

I looked high,
And I looked low.
Where did she put it?
I don't know.

Cross your hands,
Cross your hands,
Where is it now?

Hum a dum dum,
A finger or a thumb?

Stroke the baby

One child is the Baby and faces the wall. Another child strokes her back while the rest of the group say the rhyme. The child facing the wall then turns around and tries to guess who stroked her back. If she guesses right, that child becomes the Baby. If not, the first child has another turn.

UK

I looked high

One child hides a soft toy as the others count to five with their eyes shut. While they search for it, they say the rhyme. The finder hides the toy next time.

Australia, Canada, UK, USA

Cross your hands

One child shows the group a small object, then hides it in one fist, behind his back. Next, he crosses his hands in front of him as the group says the rhyme. He then asks a member of the group to guess which hand the object is hidden in.

Sri Lanka

Hum a dum dum

One child hides his face in his lap. Another child taps him on the shoulder as she says the rhyme, and ends by holding up a finger or a thumb. The first child then guesses which she is holding up. If he guesses right, he says the rhyme next time.

UK

You're It! Games

Acka backa BOO!

Count between two children or around a group, pointing to a new child with each word. Eliminate the child you are pointing to as you say "YOU." The last child left in the game wins.

Canada, UK, USA

Olika bolika

Count the feet of children sitting in a circle as you say each word of the rhyme. The child whose foot you are pointing to on "NOB" should bend his knee and tuck his foot under him. The last child with a foot still sticking out wins.

Belgium, Germany, Holland, UK

Acka Backa Soda Cracker,
Acka Backa BOO!
Acka Backa Soda Cracker,
Out Goes YOU.

Olika bolika,
Susan solika,
Olika bolika,
NOB.

Tickum-tackum,
Tickum-tackum,
Tickum-tackum,
MORE.

Up and down,
Up and down,
Up and down,
And STOP.

Ram, ram,
Ram, ram,
Ram, ram,
RIP.

Tickum-tackum
Two players walk ten feet apart, shout "tickum-tackum," and turn around. They then take turns walking forward, putting heel to toe, the first player shouting "tickum" and the second player "tackum" as they go. The child whose foot fills the final gap is the winner.

Iran, UK

Up and down
Three or more players hold hands and swing them up and down. On the word "STOP" they place their right hand on their left hand, either palm up or palm down. If there are more palms *down* than *up*, the palms *up* win and vice versa. Play continues until one child is left. If two children are left, the game is played again.

Pakistan

Ram, ram, RIP
One player holds out his hand, palm up. The others rest the tips of their index fingers on his palm. The first player says the rhyme, and on "RIP" he closes his hand quickly and tries to catch a finger. The player whose finger is caught is out. If the first player catches more than one, the game is played again.

Indonesia, Malaysia

Hands and Feet Games

Bounce and whirl around
One child says the rhyme as she bounces the ball and turns around to catch it. She counts how many times she can do this without missing, trying to beat the previous score.

Syria

Ichi, ni, san
The children hold up their fingers to match each number as they sing or say the rhyme.

Music on page 42.

Japan

With my hands
The children play by themselves or in a group, fitting the actions to the rhyme or song.

Music on page 42.

Australia, UK, USA

Bounce and whirl around,
Toes on the ground.

Ichi, ni, san,
Ni, sorekara shi, sorekara go,
San, ichi, ni, sorekara shi,
Sorekara ni, sorekara shi, sorekara go.

(One, two, three,
Two, then four, then five,
Three, one, two, then four,
Then two, then four, then five.)

With my hands I clap, clap, clap.
With my feet I tap, tap, tap.
Right foot first,
Left foot, then,
Turn around and back again.

Uno (one),
Dos (two),
Tres (three),
TIRAS! (THROW!)

Muoy (one),
Pi (two),
Bey (three),
JUMP!

Here I come
With one leg.
Watch me run,
I'll catch YOU.

Match my feet.
Copy what I do.
Just like ME.

Uno, dos, tres
Stretch a string between two objects and mark a line a yard away. Children stand behind the line and take turns throwing bean bags at the string. Any child who hits it, scores a point.

Chile

Muoy, pi, bey
Draw two parallel lines in the soil. Say the rhyme and on "JUMP" one child jumps from the starting line to the far side of the second line. Repeat the rhyme until each child has had a turn, then move the second line a little farther away. The game continues until one child is left.

Cambodia

Here I come
The catcher stands in a circle of chalk. Children hop in and out of the circle. When a player is inside the circle, the catcher can tag him using his foot. The first child caught becomes the new catcher.

Thailand

Match my feet
The children stand in a circle. The leader claps a rhythm and everyone joins in. The leader then stands in front of another child, and makes up a dance to the rhythm. If the second child copies the dance successfully, he becomes the leader. If not, the leader chooses a different child and repeats the dance.

Zaire

Catching Games

Fire on the mountain

The children lie faceup, outside a safe area known as "home." The leader pretends to look far away for fire. He says, "Fire on the mountain," and the children repeat, "Fire, fire." He then says, "Fire in the valley," and the children chorus, "Fire, fire." He continues naming places where he can see fire, until he says, "Fire right HERE." The children jump up and run for home. The last one home is out of the game.

Tanzania

Grandmother, what do you want?

The children stand behind a starting line opposite the child chosen to be Grandmother, who can have her face or back to them, depending on the children's age. The first child asks Grandmother, "What do you want?" She replies any of the following: "two giant strides," "four mouse steps," "three fairy feet," etc. The child carries out the steps, then it is the next child's turn. The child who gets close enough to Grandmother to touch her is the winner, and becomes the new Grandmother.

Belgium, Switzerland

Fire on the mountain,
Fire, fire,
Fire in the valley,
Fire, fire,
Fire right HERE.

Grandmother,
What do you want?

23

Un, deux, trois, quatre

Four children stand, one in each corner of an imaginary square, with a fifth in the middle. On "ALL CHANGE!" the children at the corners swap places, while the child in the middle tries to get into an empty corner first.

France, UK

Socorro!

A chaser runs after the children and tries to catch them. When a child is in danger of being caught, she shouts, "Socorro!" If a player comes and holds her hand, they are both safe from being caught. Once the danger is past, they continue running individually.

Peru

Taia ya taia!

The catcher shouts, *"Taia ya taia,"* and starts hopping on one foot. The other players chase him and try to tag him. As they do, he tries to tag them. Any player he touches becomes the new catcher.

Egypt

Uno, due, tre, STELLA

The leader turns her back. The other children creep up, trying to touch her. She counts to three and on *"STELLA"* turns around. Any child she sees moving has to go back to the starting line. The first child to touch her back becomes the leader.

Italy, France

24

Un (one),
Deux (two),
Trois (three),
Quatre (four),
CHANGEZ VOS PLACES! (ALL CHANGE!)

Socorro! (Help!)
Help me
QUICK!

*Taia ya
Taia!*
Tag me
If you can!

Uno (one),
Due (two),
Tre (three),
STELLA.

25

Ball Games

Queenie, Queenie
One child is chosen to be Queenie. She stands with her back to the other children and throws a ball over her head toward them. The child who picks it up hides it behind his back, and everyone says the rhyme. Queenie then turns around and guesses who has the ball. If she picks the right child, he becomes the new Queenie.

UK

Hot potato
The children sit in a circle. A beanbag or soft ball is passed around as quickly as possible, while they chant, "Hot potato." When the leader shouts, "OUT!" the child who is holding the ball is out.

Ireland, UK, USA

Queenie, Queenie,
Who's got the ball?
Is she tall or is she small,
Is she fat or is she thin,
Or does she have a double chin?

Hot potato,
Hot potato,
Hot potato,
OUT!

27

Clap, clap, clap

The children stand in two rows, a few feet apart. The first child throws a ball to someone in the other row. As he throws, all the players clap; when the ball is caught they all stamp their feet. The catcher then throws the ball back to another child. The clapping and stamping continues as the ball is thrown from one row to the other. If anyone drops the ball, it is returned to the thrower, and the game continues until the children are tired.

Cameroon

One, two, three a-leerie

Children can play alone or in a group. On the numbers in the rhyme, the child bounces the ball. On "a-leerie" she lifts one leg over the ball, then catches it. On "catch me" she bounces the ball, twirls around, and catches it.

UK

Pig in the middle

Three children make a line, and the central one is the "pig in the middle" (or any other animal you choose). The two end children throw or roll a ball to each other, saying the first two lines, and the Pig says, "Yes, I CAN!" as he tries to catch it. If the Pig gets the ball he changes places with the child who threw it.

Ireland, UK

Clap, clap, clap,
Catch the ball.
Stamp, stamp, stamp,
Who's caught the ball?

One, two, three a-leerie,
Four, five, six a-leerie,
Seven, eight, nine a-leerie,
Ten a-leerie,
Catch me.

Pig in the middle,
Can't get out.
Yes, I CAN!

Hide-and-Seek Games

Eins, zwei, drei

One child is chosen to hide. After counting to five, the rest of the children go off to search. The child who finds the hidden child hides next time.

Germany, UK

Jack, Jack, shine your light

One child is chosen to be Jack, and goes off with a flashlight anywhere in the house. The others call out the rhyme and Jack shines his flashlight in reply, once. The others try to find him, but he keeps moving. They repeat the rhyme and he shows his light from his new hiding place, and then moves again. The child who catches him becomes the next Jack.

UK

Eins (one),
Zwei (two),
Drei (three),
Vier (four),
Fünf (five),
Wir KOMMEN!
(We're COMING!)

Jack, Jack, shine your light,
Aren't you playing out tonight?

One, two, three, WHOOPS!

One child hides his eyes and counts to ten, while the others hide. When they are all hidden they shout, "WHOOPS!" The seeker tries to find them and catch them; meanwhile they try to run "home" without being seen. The first one caught becomes the new seeker.

UK

Sardines

All the players shut their eyes and say the rhyme while one child hides. As soon as a seeker finds the hiding child, he joins her in the hiding place. Play continues until all the players are squashed together in the same place, like sardines. The first child to find the hiding place hides next time.

Australia, Canada, UK

Huckle, buckle, BEANSTALK!

One child hides a small object in full view. The other children hunt for it. As soon as they see it they say, "Huckle, buckle, BEANSTALK," and sit down without looking at it. The first child to sit down hides it the next time.

USA

One, two, three, four, five, six, seven, eight, nine, ten.
Are you ready?
—WHOOPS!

Sardines in a tin,
One more to fit in.
Pull, push, squeeze,
Move up PLEASE!

Huckle, buckle,
BEANSTALK!

Clap, Skip, and Jump Games

My father went to sea

Two children face each other and clap hands together, trying not to make a mistake. Either make up your own clapping pattern or use the following:

Lines 1–3: On alternate beats, clap right then left hands together, and on the last three words clap own hands together.

Line 4: Clap own hands on each beat.

Line 5: Clap each other's hands together on "SEA, SEA, SEA."

UK

Mosquito one

This is a counting game. The children slap the floor or clap on the word "mosquito." They hold up the corrrect number of fingers as the numbers are called out, making up actions for lines 2, 4, 6, 8, and 10.

Caribbean

My father went to sea, sea, sea,
To see what he could see, see, see.
But all that he could see, see, see,
Was the bottom of the deep blue
SEA, SEA, SEA.

A mosquito one, a mosquito two,
A mosquito jump in the old man shoe,
A mosquito three, a mosquito four,
A mosquito open the old man door.
A mosquito five, a mosquito six,
A mosquito pick up the old man sticks.
A mosquito seven, a mosquito eight,
A mosquito open the old man gate.
A mosquito nine, a mosquito ten,
A mosquito biting the man again.

Higher and higher,
Up it goes,
Where it stops,
Nobody knows.

Bluebells, cockle shells,
Eevy, ivy, OVER.

Andy, Mandy,
Sugar candy,
Now's the time
To MISS!

Pina-one,
Pina-two,
Pina-three,
PINAFORE.

Higher and higher
The children see who can jump over the highest rope, chanting the rhyme at every jump. After each round, the rope is moved higher.

Morocco, UK, USA

Bluebells, cockle shells
The aim is to jump the most "overs." Two children sway the rope from side to side as the other children jump over it. When the rhyme says "OVER," they turn the rope full circle and continue turning faster and faster until someone misses.

UK

Andy, Mandy, sugar candy
Two children turn the rope for the others. Just before "MISS!" the jumping children all run out. Anyone caught by the rope becomes a rope turner, or misses a turn.

UK, USA

Pina-one
The children see who can skip four skips without missing—one on each beat of the rhyme.

Belgium, UK

Singing Games

Tootsie in da moonlight

The children stand in a circle, clapping as they sing. One child is chosen to be Tootsie, and walks around the outside of the circle as the others clap and point at her. On "Walk in" Tootsie walks into the middle, and stands and waits. Tootsie sings verse three, and as she says the name of a child in the group, this child joins Tootsie in the circle. They join hands and skip while the circle sings the last verse. Then the chosen child becomes the new Tootsie, and the game begins again.

Music on page 42.

Caribbean

Tootsie in da moonlight,
Tootsie in da dew,
Tootsie never come back
Before the clock struck two.

Walk in, Tootsie, walk in,
Walk right in I say.
Walk into my parlor
To hear my banjo play.

I don't love nobody
And nobody loves me.
All I love is Mary
To come and dance with me.

Tra la la la la la la,
Tra la la la la,
Tra la la la la la la,
Tra la la la la.

39

Che-che-koo-lay,
Che-che-koo-lay,

Che-che ko-fi sa,
Che-che ko-fi sa,

Ko-fi sa-lan-ga,
Ko-fi sa-lan-ga,

Ca-ca-shi lan-ga,
Ca-ca-shi lan-ga,

Koom a-day-day,
Koom a-day-day.

In and out of the Dusty Bluebells,
In and out of the Dusty Bluebells,
In and out of the Dusty Bluebells,
Who shall be my darling?

Pitter, patter, pitter, patter on
    your shoulders,
Pitter, patter, pitter, patter on
    your shoulders,
Pitter, patter, pitter, patter on
    your shoulders,
You shall be my darling.

Che-che-koo-lay

The children form a circle with one child in the middle who sings the first line with hands on his head. The other children copy the action. On the third line he touches his shoulders, on the fifth line his hips, and on the seventh line his ankles. Each time the other children copy him. On "Koom a-day-day" they all fall down and lie there until the child in the middle jumps up. The other children then run away and the child who is caught is the next "it."
Music on page 43.
Ghana

Dusty Bluebells

The children form a circle. Holding hands, they raise their arms to make arches. One child skips in and out of the arches, singing. At the end of the first verse she stops in front of the nearest child and pats him on alternate shoulders as she sings the second verse. That child then becomes the leader and the first child holds on to his waist as they skip under the arches.
Music on page 43.
UK

Music

The following rhymes can either be said, or sung. If you want to sing or hum them, try these easy tunes.

Ichi, ni, san

See page 19

One, two, three, Two, then four, then five,
Ichi, ni, san, Ni, sorekara shi, sorekara go,

three, One, two, then four, Then two, then four, then five.
San, ichi, ni, sorekara shi, Sorekara ni, sorekara shi, sorekara go.

With my hands

See page 19

With my hands I clap, clap, clap. With my feet I tap, tap, tap.

Right foot first, Left foot, then Turn a-round and back a-gain.

Tootsie in da moonlight

See page 38

Toot-sie in da moon-light, Toot-sie in da dew,

Toot-sie ne-ver come back be-fore the clock struck two.

Che-che-Koo-lay

See page 40

Che-che-koo-lay, Che-che-koo-lay, Che-che ko-fi sa, Che-che ko-fi sa,

Ko-fi sa-lan-ga, Ko-fi sa-lan-ga, Ca-ca-shi lan-ga, Ca-ca-shi lan-ga,

Koom a-day-day, Koom a-day-day.

The Dusty Bluebells

See page 41

In and out of the Dus-ty Blue-bells, In and out of the Dus-ty Blue-bells,

In and out of the Dusty Blue-bells, Who shall be my dar-ling?

Verse 2 begins :

Pit-ter, pat-ter, pit-ter, pat-ter

43

10 tips to help you run the games

1. The first time you play a game, simplify it and speak slowly, taking part as both organizer and player. This way, children can learn by listening as well as watching.

2. End a game by summing up and giving some praise for effort. Try to play the same game again immediately, as children like a second chance to improve their play.

3. Each time you play a game, follow the same routine, so children can put all their concentration into getting better at it.

4. Children need new challenges, so, as they develop skills, introduce new games or add more complicated rules to games they already know.

5. If children are reluctant to join in, encourage them to do so, and when they do, make sure they have fun. With luck, they'll want to play next time!

6. In games where children are eliminated, make sure that when they are out they don't get bored. Have a special task for them to do or ask them to help you run the game.

7. Look for extra opportunities to talk to children while you play. Try giving a running commentary on how the game is going and what someone is doing.

8. As children get to know a game well, they may be capable of running it themselves. Stay around at first, in case they need a little help from you.

9. Success is vital for motivation. Encourage and be positive: negative remarks are not constructive and can break bonds. Praise participation, effort, and achievement, as well as actual winning, but remember children are critical of unjustified praise.

10. Games are about having fun, and you can put a lot of fun into them. Add suspense by the varying way you use your voice and your actions. Be playful, and sometimes more daring than the children expect. It all adds to everyone's enjoyment.

Index of Games

These games are known to be played in the following places:

Australia, Belgium, Cambodia, Cameroon, Canada, Caribbean, Chile, Egypt, France, Germany, Ghana, Holland, India, Indonesia, Iran, Ireland, Italy, Japan, Malaysia, Morocco, Pakistan, Peru, Sri Lanka, Switzerland, Syria, Tanzania, Thailand, UK, USA, Zaire.

They may also be played elsewhere around the world.

Pronunciation Guide

Hindi on page 10
Andar	Under
Bahar	Baa-har

Japanese on page 19
Ichi	Ee-chee
Ni	Nee
San	San
Sorekara	So-ray-car-ah
Shi	She
Go	Go

Spanish on page 20
Uno	Oono
Dos	Dos
Tres	Trace
Tiras	Tee-rass

Khmer on page 20
Muoy	Moo-eey
Pi	Pee
Bey	Buy

French on page 24
Un	Uhn
Deux	Duh
Trois	Twah
Quatre	Catr
Changez	Shon-zhay
Vos	Vo
Places	Plahss

Spanish on page 24
Socorro	So-koro

Egyptian on page 25
Taia	Taya
Ya	Yah

Italian on page 25
Uno	Oono
Due	Doo-ay
Tre	Tray
Stella	Stay-la

German on page 30
Eins	Eynts
Zwei	Tsvai
Drei	Dry
Vier	Fear
Fünf	Fuunf
Wir	Veer
Kommen	Co-mun

Ghanaian on page 40
Che	Cheh
Koo	Koo
Lay	Lay
Ko	Ko
Fi	Fee
Sa	Sah
Lan	Lahn
Ga	Gah
Ca	Kah
Shi	She
Koom	Koom
A	Ah
Day	Day